The Virtue of Patients

Advice From Clients

Minerva Spurlock Ph.D.

Voynich Press

ISBN 978-1-963882-00-1 (Hard Cover)

ISBN 978-1-963882-10-0 (Paperback)

ISBN 978-1-963882-02-5 (Audio Book)

ISBN 978-1-963882-09-4 (E-book)

Voynich Press LLC, Tiffin, Ohio

Printed in the United States of America

Cover design by Minerva Spurlock

Dedication

I wish to thank all my patients who chose to participate in this
altruistic adventure.
Thank you for having the courage to share your insights and
perspectives with the world.

Contents

Introduction

Every single one of us has a collection of thoughts, beliefs, opinions, ideals, perspectives, and worldviews that are formed based on our experiences, knowledge, and geographical location.

At the end of the day, not only do I hope to facilitate self-growth in my patients, but I also strive to be the best version of myself. My goal is not to teach my patients certain concepts or ideas, but rather to create a space in which they can think about their thoughts from a perspective outside of their own.

As a doctor with a background in clinical psychology, I align with a humanistic approach, I promote self-discovery, and achieving one's full potential. In sessions, I follow the lead of my patients as I feel they know themselves better than I ever could. It is with this perspective I am continuously able to learn in a non-judgmental and empathetic manner.

~ Minerva Spurlock Ph.D.

Chapter One

Therapeutic Lessons

Happiness is a choice.

It is not something you should seek out, it is something you should create.

My grandma once told me happiness is a direction you aim for in life; she was one of the smartest women I had the pleasure of knowing.

I have discovered that my happiness may look different than your happiness, and that is okay.

-Patient 52

I've learned how to talk through things.

Therapy is about what "I" say/think and not what the therapist tells me.

I cannot control how other people live and/or react - even if I think I am helping.

-Patient 85

One of the primary lessons I learned in therapy was being mindful of how I relate to individuals in whatever situation I am in – I place myself in the other person's shoes. Would I relate in similar songs e.g., being kind when I could be gruff, remaining silent when related to in a hurting way, being positive in my attitudes, and being patient, kind, and understanding? God did not make us to be perfect individuals. Jesus was not perfect, but He came to show us the way.

-Patient 33

Live with no regrets.

-Patient 95

I was diagnosed right before I turned 50. That answered so, so, many questions. Why did other children call me names and call me dumb? I couldn't understand why. I got good grades in school. Sometimes, some of the things they did and the way they acted scared me. Why even when I was an adult I didn't understand other adults. I learned to act like other people, even though I had no idea of what it really meant. There are so many rules to remember.

I have always known that I was different. I didn't like myself because I wasn't like everyone else. After my diagnosis, it gave me the answers I needed. I have a grandson that is autistic so I have done some research on it. That was what made me want to be tested. I have learned that it's more than OK to be me and it is more than OK to see the world the way I do.

I have learned that I have found the perfect doctor. I hope it is OK to talk about her. I haven't asked first. Dr. Spurlock (Minerva) has introduced me to myself. I hope she knows how much I've loved my journey so far and I look forward to my future now.

I finally like myself now, after a long life of feeling 'less than' other people. It is OK to be different. You should never try to be "normal". What is "normal" anyway?

-Patient 117

Learn about your worldview.

We all have them, even if you don't know what yours is or how to define it.

-Patient 60

Never stop learning.

We constantly have things and people around us that act as teachers if we allow them.

Learning is about self-growth and it is one of the keys to living a happy life. Of course sometimes when we are learning something it is difficult and frustrating. Those tough times though can make the achievement of reaching whatever goal is on the table even more worthwhile.

Never give up. Keep trying.

-Patient 149

Life is a journey, not a destination.

Before Aerosmith decided to use this saying as a line in their song *'Amazing'*, Ralph Waldo Emerson coined the phrase that became a well-known, often-repeated inspirational quote.

For me, this saying is about cherishing every second of every minute of every hour of every day. If you think about it, we are all on different journeys. Over 8 billion people on this planet and we each have our own unique journey – that is a mind-boggling thought.

-Patient 4

Chapter Two

Life Lessons

A life lesson I learned is that I judged myself so harshly because of all the abuse and what I was "taught" by my abusers. Learning to accept myself has helped my depression so much that I have been able to go off some of my depression and nightmare medications.

-Patient 29

When I was studying and practicing massage therapy many years ago, some of my classmates and I volunteered at a nursing home facility in Santa Fe, New Mexico. As we were being shown through the facility one of the nurses said it would be better not to go in a particular man's room – he was liable to up and hit us and his language was atrocious.

One week I was going into various rooms trying to bring love and comfort to the person at hand. When I entered a particular room and realized I was in the place we were warned not to go. I couldn't back out now so I went up to the old gentleman and asked if I could do a simple massage of perhaps his arms, neck, or whatever he felt comfortable with.

Gruffly he asked, "How much will it cost?"

I said, "There is no charge."

"Oh." was his response. So I began a gentle massage to his arms. I noticed some pictures on the wall of his room. One looked like a church so I asked him if this was the church he used to go to. He said, "Yes," and that "it was located in Taos."

A nurse came into the room, said nothing, and just looked at the two of us. As I finished what I was doing and was about to leave this gentleman's room he said to me, "God bless you." I felt so honored – he never said a derogatory word and was so gentle. I wish I could have followed up on this new acquaintance. I believe all he needed was a gentle caring touch and a listening ear. This proved to me what a bit of kindness can do in the life of another and in mine too.

One evening I entered the massage session with my client in the usual manner with a prayer and focusing on the needs of the body. All was seemingly going well when all of a sudden the client sat up on the table and began to sob. At first, I was taken aback.

I sat beside him as he poured out his fears and sorrows regarding how he had raised his children. I listened intently and assured him he had done his best, but suggested he talk over the matter with his minister or priest. He seemed to regain his composure and was more at peace.

This episode taught me that the help of God and the knowledge of varying team members are needed to continue life's journey in a spirit of peace and calm.

-Patient 176

Try replacing every negative thought you have with a positive one.
It is healthier to have a positive mindset rather than a negative one.

-Patient 17

Treat children with love and kindness. My grandchildren love me for who I am and how I treat them. I am truthful and let them know that I don't know how to play pretend. They accept it and we just play something else like the floor is ice or lava, or they help me do what I need to do. The important thing is to make them feel special, wanted, and needed. Let them know that they can trust you. I made sure to do that for my grandchildren. I want to do that for them; it was what my dad did for me.

-Patient 56

There is one important lesson I've learned in life:

> "Life is a journey that must be traveled, no matter how
> bad the roads or accommodations."
>
> -Oliver Goldsmith

Our journey begins with one step, not towards your destination, but towards the changes you are either looking for or to make. In the Netflix original series, BoJack Horseman, BoJack once said:

> *"In the great grand scheme of things, we are just tiny*
> *specs that will one day be forgotten. So it does not matter*
> *what we did in the past, or how we will be remembered.*
> *The only thing that matters is right now, this moment."*
> BoJack Horseman. Season 3 Episode 11

Yes, everyone's life is essential, however, no matter the fame, fortune, or ethnicity someone has, we are all still just people. We are people who will be loved, hated, and eventually forgotten. In the grand scheme of things, our lives are but tiny specs in this world. Focus on your journey and enjoy the life you have now.

> -Patient 188

I think it is important to remember we have all been through things.
Before you judge someone, remember that you do not know everything that is going on in their life.

-Patient 15

I have learned that sometimes when people say something negative or judgmental, their words are a reflection of their insecurities and struggles.

-Patient 111

Chapter Three

Advice to Share

Hello, Here's my advice.

When your son or daughter is dating someone you can't stand, let the relationship run its course. They eventually dump the person anyway.

Speaking from experience my parents got involved and tried to force a breakup between a guy and me. It did not work and created resentment towards my parents. About a year later I lost feelings for him and dumped him anyway.

-Patient 45

A piece of advice I would like to share is that life is short. Put God first and love, enjoy, and appreciate your family. Always tell them how much they mean and how much you love them.

-Patient 73

Similar to tides, life ebbs and flows. It's about balance and moderation. Finding a balance that works for you in your life is important. Balance and moderation can help you appreciate things that already exist in your life. When life gets tough, it can be helpful to remember that easier times may be coming sooner than you think.

-Patient 61

Read as much as you can.

The more you read, the more opportunities you have to experience the writings of some of the greatest minds of all time. Reading benefits people in a multitude of ways: professionally, creatively, romantically, emotionally, physically, and personally. Readers who do so regularly tend to sleep better and have higher levels of self-esteem than non-regular readers.

Reading can strengthen our critical thinking skills and help us learn more about certain topics before we make a decision or judgment. Reading a physical book can provide a healthy escape from the world of technology that continues to increasingly grow. Reading can help us decompress and decrease our stress levels. Reading has the potential to inspire us to achieve goals we never thought possible.

-Patient 123

Be the change you want to see in the world. It costs nothing to smile at someone or offer a genuine compliment to someone you are passing by.

-Patient 177

Take responsibility for your actions. If you make a mistake, learn from it and try not to repeat it. Remember that our mistakes are lessons in progress. Life is about having the courage to not be perfect and learn from its lessons.

-Patient 82

If I was going to share a piece of advice it would be relating to the concept of control: what we can control and what we cannot control.

It is not your job to control how someone else reacts to something you do or say. Your job is to be the most authentic version of yourself. You live your experiences and allow others to live theirs. Your feelings are valid, just as are everyone else's.

You are in control of your responses and no one else's. You manage you. Let everyone else manage everyone else.

-Patient 24

Chapter Four

Wish You Knew Sooner

My identity.

For me, quite simply, I wish I had understood my identity sooner. I thought I knew exactly who I was and what I was about until I was 37 years old. Straight, white woman who would like to have children, although marriage seemed daunting as part of that process. One comment on social media in response to a statement that I made about just wanting "Someone who will be my companion. Someone that goes to events with me, but mainly just hangs out watching movies and playing video games with me at home" sent me down a rabbit hole.

They identified as asexual and could relate to my wants, while others in a personality type group could not relate. It did not take long to figure out why I was 37 with no real long-term relationships under my belt. Not only asexual, but aromantic too? My life as far back as my first crush, began to make complete sense. I never wanted to make out with him or anything, I just wanted to hang out with him because he was genuinely nice and I found him aesthetically attractive. Imagine, though...if I had known sooner...I wouldn't be who I am today, but wow I would have skipped a lot of discomfort (mentally and physically) in my 20s and 30s.

-Patient 80

This is a lesson I wish I had known sooner. My life was hard. The abuses I had suffered left me so confused about how to share my love. I didn't think I was worthy of love.

-Patient 100

Always be learning.

Whether it be a structured schooling situation or just hearing a new term and looking it up, take the time to learn. I will either learn something about another human experience and/or realize my own.

-Patient 161

The perspective of failure as a positive thing. Failure gives us a chance to learn and grow from different experiences. It should not define us as individuals, but rather it should help shape us into who we want to be.

Failure teaches us to be adaptable and flexible. It creates opportunities for us to learn how to conquer various obstacles and challenges. Failure helps us see the success in our progress; it creates chances for us to work on our resilience.

Failure can show us what we are missing and help us become better humans. Without failures in our lives, we would be less kind and compassionate. Without failures, we would not take as many chances as we currently do.

Does failure hurt? Absolutely.

Is it something we can get through? Absolutely.

Most of us learned to walk, speak, or write at some point and it wasn't something that happened overnight. Those milestones sometimes take years. But we did it, and we failed numerous times, and we continued to do it until we achieved the goal we were aiming for.

Failure gives us experience, knowledge, growth, and resilience.

-Patient 22

If you can't say something nice, you don't need to say anything. We all have enough stuff going on in our lives; we don't need negativity sprinkled on top.

-Patient 3

I wish I had known sooner that I needed to hold myself accountable. There are times when no one is watching and I am fighting my battles on my own. I have learned I must stay within my boundaries of morality and act with integrity.

Holding myself accountable has helped me at work and at home. I can tell my levels of anxiety and stress have decreased significantly, which I am grateful for.

-Patient 46

Practice forgiveness. Forgive others and most importantly, forgive yourself.

-Patient 74

Chapter Five

Secrets of Thriving in This Lifetime

Always be changing :)

Be willing to accept when you're wrong, listen to new opinions/beliefs, and be open to the fact that the way you are isn't the only and/or best way. How it always was doesn't have to be how it always will be.

-Patient 130

Don't ever forget those who love you every day. Forget the past that makes you cry and focus on the other things that make you smile. Forget the pain, but never forget the lessons you gained, and always remember that you can learn something new every day.

Some people out there will quit on you! But you got to get up every day and make sure you never quit on yourself. Nobody knows the real me... Nobody knows how many times I've sat in my room and cried; how many times I've lost hope; how many times I've been let down even by those who are close to me; how many times I have felt like I was going to snap; and how many times I have had to hold back my tears.

Sometimes the strongest people are the ones who love beyond all faults. I have cried behind closed doors and fought battles that nobody knows or can even imagine. Only those who have gone through the darkness of times can truly appreciate the light. From one day to the next, I never know which version of myself I am going to be.

You have to stop worrying about what other people think of you and focus on yourself instead.

Focus on what makes you happy. Focus on what makes your soul feel at peace. You are your biggest commitment, so start loving your flaws, your awkwardness, your weirdness, your intensity, and your vulnerability. Life becomes so much more fulfilling when you are simply yourself.

The world keeps spinning whether people understand you or not, so why not make this next trip around the Sun about yourself. There are some days I can cook and the next day, I can't even remember how to cook or how to handle the next situation without help. It's always repetitive, repetitive, repetitive for me. I have to do the same things every single day or I can get frustrated. I have learned that there are 1 million ways to do something, you just have to find the one way that works for you. Like taking a house bill that is $137.80 and making it $140.00. Before you can accomplish your goals, you have to take the time and figure out what you will and won't stand for and who you are as a person. Most of the time you just have to take one step at a time and just do what comes naturally to you, whether it's wrong or right.

I have also learned that sometimes you can't back down because you are afraid; you have to figure out how to get even instead. I have also learned that God only gives you what he knows that you can handle. You are always going to have a target on your back, but you are going to have to figure out who you can trust.

-Patient 49

You will learn more out of school, than in school. Don't ever let anyone degrade you for being yourself. Who cares what other people think of you as long as you are happy with yourself. That is all that matters. You are going to find out that a lot of people aren't going to like you because you are different and you are not normal, but in my book who is normal because normal is overrated. Just remember to stay true to yourself only and don't worry about anyone else.

-Patient 101

I think a secret to thriving in this lifetime is to love God first. Look for the good in life and the good in each day.

-Patient 7

I try to be the best me that I can be, by not trying to be like someone else, and by not trying to have what someone else has. I never wish I could be anyone else but who I am. Be who you are, not who someone else wants you to be.

-Patient 99

Mindfulness.

I have been practicing it on a daily basis. Sometimes I meditate, sometimes I do something in a mindful manner, like do the dishes.

I have been keeping the word 'Mindful' in the forefront of my mind, training my brain to remember it more often.

I feel like I am able to be more present and more self-aware, which is progress in my book.

-Patient 172

It is okay to ask for help. We have all needed it at one time or another.

Asking for help is a sign that you are mindful and resourceful. It is also a sign of confidence and strength.

Asking for help could save lives. It can set an example and inspire others to do the same when they feel they need help.

-Patient 21

Chapter Six

Being the Best Version of Yourself

I don't believe that I ever will be the best version of myself. If I'm at my best, what is left to do in this life? I'll be lucky to reach that version of myself before the day that I die. I think I'll always be learning and evolving.

-Patient 138

Live for today.

Dwelling on the past or obsessing about the future is a vicious cycle. We can't do anything about either of those things in our current moment.

-Patient 79

My sister can be hard to get along with and deal with, but she has taught me a lot of different things that my mother and my aunt wouldn't have thought about teaching me like how to defend myself and who I can and can't trust. I don't know what I would do if she weren't in my life, even when it seems that I'm not important to her sometimes.

My aunt has done a lot for me, even when I don't always deserve it. Even now we butt heads sometimes and she doesn't always trust me. As for my mother, we have been through a lot together and I wouldn't want anyone but her as a mother. However, she can be very, very overprotective when it comes to me. I wish sometimes she would let go and see if I can pick myself up and keep going.

-Patient 103

Ride the Waves.

As someone with a panic disorder, my anxiety often doesn't have a life event or trigger specifically. Sometimes, that is how things are. These feelings rise and fall for a reason or no reason at all. We can't control everything and some days we just have to ride the waves of life and mental illness. The harder we fight it, the more it will wear us down until we are so far underwater that we can't get out on our own. In those situations, call your lifeguard therapist and schedule a session, but hopefully, after learning how, we can surf on our own!

-Patient 14

Even though bad decisions can make good stories, you should weigh the pros and cons before you follow through with anything.

-Patient 166

I think for me to be the best version of myself, I have to continue to be driven by internal motivations rather than external ones. Once I learned about the differences between intrinsic and extrinsic motivations I understood myself on a deeper level.

Intrinsic motivation is when you do something because you find it satisfying and rewarding. The behavior itself is the reward. For me, a good example of this is studying a subject I find interesting. I enjoy learning new things. I get pleasure from learning new things.

Extrinsic motivation is when you do something because you want to avoid punishment or earn a reward. So you do something not because you enjoy it, but because you expect to get something in return. An example of this would be someone studying because they want a good grade.

If you can align your goals with intrinsic motivations, it will help you a lot.

-Patient 91

I have learned that attitude really is everything. How we choose to respond to something or someone is crucial. I have learned that I can say what I need to say without raising my voice. When I am mindful of how I say what I want to say, it is more respectful to everyone involved in the conversation.

-Patient 32

Chapter Seven

Additional Thoughts and Opinions

Children need more protection from bullies, mostly in school in this day and age.

Cherish the time you have with your children in your life. Life is so short. You never know what a child has to live through, so cherish them when you can.

Always say "I love you" to your loved ones and show your love to them.

-Patient 150

I am a mom of four and a grandma of nine. My children all married amazing people. I married a great guy in November 2015. I think my next-to-the-oldest grandson was diagnosed with autism in 2013 as a toddler. I did not know anything about autism. His mother sent me a link to a website with lots of information. The more I learned, the more I related to what I was learning. Fast forward to 2020. I had found a doctor that tested adults. I was diagnosed right before my 50th birthday. That was three years ago.

I have learned so much since then, most importantly I have learned that I am not alone. There are so many others who similarly view the world. I always thought there was something wrong with me. I had suffered years of abuse starting as a small child. My doctors and therapists thought it all stemmed from that. I was on a lot of medication for years. My diagnosis and having just the right doctor changed my entire world.

-Patient 39

Set goals for yourself that you can achieve. Set long-term ones and short-term ones. If you get stuck on a goal or don't reach a deadline that you initially set, do not give up or get frustrated. Simply adjust your goal and break it down into smaller, more manageable steps if you need to.

-Patient 8

Practice kindness with boundaries. Doing something kind for someone can be a great thing, like helping someone who is struggling to get their groceries in their car. Be aware of your boundaries though and make sure you aren't compromising yourself simply to please others. Learn how to say no if someone is asking too much of you.

-Patient 23

I'm going to say some things that you probably haven't heard many others say, because throughout my own healing journey, one of the most invalidating things was being told the same advice repeatedly in the same way.

I can't blame people for giving the advice they do inherently, because they have good intentions and they're trying to help, but it's hard to understand being at the darkest parts of your mind without actually being there. While everyone struggles from time to time, not everyone can understand the hopelessness that attempts to take away every last ounce of happiness that you ever had within your lifetime and make it feel so out of reach.

That feeling isn't easy to understand if you've never experienced it, as with many things, and while I'd never wish that on my worst enemy, I wish there was an easier way to cross that bridge. I don't know if there is, because experience is a teacher that teaches like no other.

However, to go back to my main point, when you're at the bottom of the ocean, the darkest depths of the cave, the last thing you want to hear is to just swim to the surface, to just.. find your way out. Go on walks, make yourself some tea, take a bath, meditate, connect with a support group, journal, attempt to look yourself in the eyes, and tell yourself how beautiful you look. And I'm not denying those things can be helpful, but told this straight off the bat without anything else can feel discouraging, especially if you've already done those things, and still don't really "feel better".

When I'm told to go on a walk, to do all those things I listed, it feels like the person who told that to me doesn't really see me as a person. They see my negative emotions as an inconvenience, something in the way with the ultimate goal of "getting better" because dealing with all of that junk is a waste of their time. It's left up to me to get better through all of these things that I hardly have the energy to do, as if I didn't come for your help because I couldn't figure it all out in the first place. Because I couldn't fight it on my own.

When I'm told to change my perspective and change my thoughts and my feelings, I feel as though I'm taking away one of the last pieces of myself that I had left from my childhood. That the safety I've become adjusted to with the pain is as easy as closing my eyes and watching a YouTube tutorial on how to make my life better. So obviously, I'm not going to tell you that.

Instead, I'm going to tell you something else.

Sometimes, it's ok for things to just, suck. It's ok for things to just be bad, to just sit and sulk and rot in yourself for a while. Sometimes it's ok to just sit and cry and not function like society wants you to. This world can be absolutely horrible, brutal, and cruel. And denying that can feel even worse than the wound itself. In the same metaphor, healing can be worse than the wound itself. The recovery from surgery is worse than the surgery itself.

It's ok for healing to not be easy, it's ok for healing to be the hardest most difficult, horrific thing you've ever had to face in your life. It doesn't need to be an inherently positive or enriching experience because that's not what healing is meant to be.

The goal of healing, the TRUE goal of healing, isn't to make it all better, isn't to go back to how you were before, and it's not even to make you happy.

The goal is to make yourself just a little better than the day before. To be able to look yourself in the eyes and say, "Maybe.. just maybe, I deserve to be here. I deserve to take up space in this world." Or maybe, closer to the start, it could simply be. "I will live today, and that might be all I can do."

Everything in this world is so fast-paced, and the mental health journey gets wrapped under the same boat, and it doesn't get nearly as talked about. Yes, people make their lives look glamorized, and that's a problem of its own, but trying to heal yourself is just as glamorized. It can feel like people don't want to hear about your suffering, they only want to hear about it once you've gotten through that suffering. Once you're not at the point of extremes, a lot of people just expect you to be "happy", even if you're not.

I'm sorry that you were dealt the bad hand of life, because let's be realistic, if you decided to pick up this book, you probably were dealt one of the worst hands of all. No matter what happened, you deserved better than that. And most of all, you deserve to be happy, or maybe, just a little happier than the day before.

-Patient 114

My counselor has been helping me with my follow-through and learning how to finish what I start. This month I've finished the entire series of LOST on Amazon Prime and today I've finished 4 packages of Little Debbie Unicorn Cakes.

-Patient 87

I have learned to speak with my partner with respect and appreciation. There is a world of difference now when we disagree on something. I have learned that disagreeing is okay and that we aren't always going to see things eye-to-eye.

I have been practicing my appreciation with my partner. If I notice he scoops the cat boxes for me while I am at work, I make sure to say "thank you". I have been making it a habit to point out certain small things he does for me that I am grateful for.

I have made it a personal goal to compliment or voice my appreciation at least once a day to my partner. I feel like we are closer than ever before.

-Patient 11

I wish more people had patience.

I have learned that patience helps me be more open to new experiences and have deeper levels of empathy and discipline. It seems the more I work on myself, the more satisfaction I gain from life.

Patience strengthens my ability to be more cooperative and forgiving, which in turn, decreases my levels of stress and anxiety. The one thing we have control over is ourselves. Practicing patience combines internal and external factors to create a present mindset of interpretations.

I bet patient people tend to encounter a smaller number of negative emotions. When you have the coping skill of patience in your tool kit, you are better equipped to deal with strenuous and anxious moments.

The great thing is anyone can cultivate patience. Practicing mindfulness, gratitude, kindness, and thinking before speaking are all ways to help strengthen your patience.

-Patient 44

About the author

Minerva Nichole Spurlock holds a Ph.D. in clinical psychology. Her passion as a writer continues to flourish in literature and music. Her involvements and travels have allowed her to experience: 212 cemeteries, 93 libraries, 34 golf courses, 6 continents, and 1 orthopedic surgeon.

She currently divides her time between work, traveling, writing, reading, and cuddling with her kitties: Gizmo Turducken V, Charizard Chalupa Charlie III, Starlight Kitten-Chow McWhiskerson IV, Luna Starbright Kitten-Chow McWhiskerson III, and Callie Fiffinella Teakwood.